Intermediate Dressage

By R. L. V. ffrench Blake

DRESSAGE FOR BEGINNERS
INTERMEDIATE DRESSAGE

Intermediate Dressage
Work at Second and Third Levels

R. L. V. ffrench Blake

Illustrations by Richard Scollins
Foreword by John H. Fritz

HOUGHTON MIFFLIN COMPANY BOSTON

First American edition 1977

Copyright © 1976, 1977 by R.L.V. ffrench Blake

All rights reserved. No part of this work may be reproduced or transmitted in any form or by any means, electronic or mechanical, including photocopying and recording, or by any information storage or retrieval system, except as may be expressly permitted by the 1976 Copyright Act or in writing from the publisher. Requests for permission should be addressed in writing to Houghton Mifflin Company, 2 Park Street, Boston, Massachusetts 02108.

Library of Congress Cataloging in Publication Data

ffrench Blake, R L V
   Intermediate dressage.

   First published in 1976 under title: Elementary dressage.
   1. Dressage. I. Title.
SF309.5.F48   1977   798′.23   77-10441
ISBN 0-395-25406-X

Printed in the United States of America

M 10 9 8 7 6 5

Published in Great Britain under the title *Elementary Dressage.*

Preface

In *Dressage for Beginners* I attempted to produce an introduction to Dressage for those who wished to make a start on this fascinating side of horsemanship. I explained the basic requirements, the sequence of priorities in early schooling, the point of view of the judge in tests and many of the technical terms involved.

In this book I hope to help the rider with a First Level horse to progress toward the next stage and to give some idea of how to appreciate, as a spectator, the more advanced standards. Once again, I do not attempt to teach the reader how to ride; this is the task of the Instructor; but in setting out the priorities, and expanding on some particular aspects of schooling, I hope perhaps to help the reader toward some further progress in the right direction.

It will be a help to the reader if *Dressage for Beginners* has already been studied; but there is sufficient recapitulation of the novice stage of training in this book to enable the work to stand on its own.

I owe a particular debt to Mrs. Charles Sivewright, who took the manuscript of this book on her holiday, read it and returned it full of valuable comment and criticism; to Derek and Claude Allhusen for encouragement and advice; and to Richard Scollins, who drew the pictures.

R. L. V. ff B

Foreword

R. L. V. FFRENCH BLAKE'S *Dressage for Beginners,* first published in Great Britain and more recently in an American edition, met a crying need in the English-speaking world, where dressage training and competition have gained acceptance and popularity only in recent years, for a book aimed at beginning dressage riders and trainers in a language they could understand. Now, in this excellent sequel to that book, he has produced an equally clear and useful guide for the growing number of individuals in America who are training horses to, and competing at, the Second and Third Levels, which are roughly equivalent to the British Elementary Standards.

The book, which illustrates in detail the additional demands made on horse and rider as they advance beyond the lowest levels of training, should also prove useful to those aspiring to become dressage judges and might even be used as a text in some of the many Learner Judges' Programs developing in all parts of the country, for Colonel ffrench Blake takes the reader step by step through a Second Level dressage ride as seen from the judge's view, explaining the reasons for the judge's decisions.

With his chapter "On Watching Dressage" and his appendix, "A Spectator's Guide to Advanced Movements," the author has added useful material for the increasing number of spectators who are finding dressage an enjoyable equestrian competition to watch and who want to understand better what it is all about and why the judge(s) makes the decisions he does.

Once again, Colonel ffrench Blake, a noted British dressage authority, in a clear, informative, and imaginative way has provided a volume that meets a decided need in what some have said is the fastest growing equestrian sport in America today.

John H. Fritz

Contents

Illustrations

Intermediate Dressage

Chapter 1

The Requirements

ONCE MORE I make no apology for starting the first chapter by repeating the F.E.I. definition of Dressage and the qualities required of the horse.

1. The object of Dressage is the harmonious development of the physique and ability of the horse. As a result it makes the horse calm . . . supple . . . confident, attentive and keen, thus achieving perfect understanding with his rider.
2. These qualities are revealed by:
   a. The freedom and regularity of the paces;
   b. The harmony, lightness, and ease of the movements;
   c. The lightness of the forehand, and the engagement of the hindquarters, originating in a lively impulsion;
   d. The acceptance of the bridle, with submissiveness throughout and without any tenseness or resistance.
3. The horse thus gives the impression of doing of his own accord what is required of him. Confident and attentive he submits generously to the control of his rider, remaining absolutely straight in any movement on a straight line and bending accordingly when moving on curved lines.
4. His walk is regular, free and unconstrained. His trot is free, supple, regular, sustained and active. His canter is united, light and cadenced. His quarters are never inactive or sluggish. They respond to the slightest indication of the rider and thereby give life and spirit to all the rest of his body.
5. By virtue of a lively impulsion and the suppleness of his joints, free from the paralyzing effects of resistance, the horse obeys willingly and without hesitation and responds to the various aids calmly and with precision . . .
6. In all his work, even at the halt, the horse must be "on the bit." A horse is "on the bit" when the hocks are correctly placed, the

neck is more or less raised and arched according to the stage of training and the extension or collection of the pace, and he accepts the bridle with a light and soft contact, and submissiveness throughout. The head should remain in a steady position, as a rule slightly in front of the vertical, with a supple poll as the highest point of the neck, and no resistance should be offered to the rider.

Remembering that it is vital not to move on to the next stage before the previous one is satisfactory, the sequence for training the horse up to First Level is as follows:

First, the aim must be to achieve relaxation, the horse going calmly forward under the rider, attending to the rider and not looking about from side to side, with no attempts to dash off or hurry. The rider should be able to release and retake the reins without the horse altering speed at any pace. The horse should be able to stay in an area defined by low boards, even when ridden on a loose rein at trot or canter.

Arising out of this first essential is the second — correct gait with regular rhythm at each pace. The horse has a naturally correct gait when he is moving free without a rider. The effect of the rider's weight, exaggerated sometimes by mismanagement of the aids (reins, legs, and balance), will be to upset this rhythm, especially if the horse is pulling or resisting in any way. Until relaxation is achieved, rhythm will not be found.

Third, we must restore the free forward movement, which will also be inhibited by the arrival of the rider's weight on the horse's back. The important element in the training at this stage will be to establish an immediate response from the horse to the aids to go forward — voice, legs, seat, spur, and whip. The foundations for this are best laid by correct work on the lunge, where a combination of the voice and the whip, applied where it is most effective — on the hocks — will condition the horse to a ready response to the voice; this aid will prove invaluable when the rider is on top. The author's experience is that when this work on the lunge is cut short (probably because an amenable animal allows itself to be backed and mounted without much resistance), the penalty is generally paid in sluggish and unresponsive reaction to the aids to go forward at a later stage. The rider must insist on *immediate* response to the leg aid, by an instant sharp tap of the whip to counter reluctance at any stage of the lesson. So often riders are afraid to apply the whip sharply enough, either from a feeling of kindness or from fear of provoking reaction in the form of a buck. As a result the horse (like a child defying a parent who threatens but withholds punishment) soon finds that he can safely ignore the leg aid. In fact, ceaseless flapping and drumming on the horse's side with the legs may well deaden the response rather than improve it.

The fourth requirement at this stage is straightness. The horse must be absolutely straight at all times when traveling, or when halted on a straight line. A tendency to carry the quarters inward when cantering must be carefully avoided. When riding in a school, remember that the horse is wedge-shaped, narrower at the shoulders than across the quarters. The rider should therefore avoid the temptation to "cling to the wall," as this may well force the horse to carry himself with "quarters in."

During early training the rider will begin to improve the horse's suppleness, asking for correct bends in the corners and on any curves. It is often at this point that most resistance will be met, since all horses are stiff on one side or the other. This resistance will always disappear in time if the rider persists. The reduction of lateral resistance to the bend will pave the way to the achievement of "vertical" flexion at the poll and the rounding of the back — the hallmark of the schooled horse, when combined with lively and active paces.

Once the horse begins to flex at the poll without resistance, without opening his mouth, and without loss of rhythm or energy in the paces, it can be said to be "accepting the bit."

(A light champing or chewing at the bit is permissible.) The rider will aim to maintain the correct attitude at every pace, including the halt, and especially during transitions between one pace and another. This point in preliminary schooling represents the breakthrough into dressage proper, and until this stage is reached, the rider should have no thought of presenting the horse in a test before a judge. Many riders, unfortunately, enter the test arena without having achieved these minimum requirements, and a painful experience it can be for the judge, who longs to ring the bell and cry, "Take it away and find out what is really wanted!"

Training Level dressage tests demand that the horse should show good "working-paces" (of which more later), free walk on a long rein — circles of 20 meters diameter at trot and canter — and progressive transitions, e.g., from trot to halt through a few paces of walk.

First Level demands circles of 10 meters diameter — serpentines at the trot — lengthened strides at the trot and canter.

At Second Level the additional requirements will be circles of 10 meters at trot and canter, transitions generally less progressive than at First Level, and shoulder-in.

The rein-back has not been included in tests at this standard, but it should certainly be included in schooling; a horse that cannot rein back is of little use as a hack or a hunter, and the rein-back is of great value as an indication of the progress of the horse's suppleness and use of the back and hindquarters. However, it should not be overdone.

At Third Level the requirements are altogether much more severe: collection and extension in all three gaits — working paces replaced by medium or collected — circles of 8 meters at trot and canter — shoulder-in, travers, renvers, and half-pass at trot — rein-back — counter-canter and simple change through the walk — transitions no longer progressive but direct from walk to canter and vice versa.

These requirements indicate a great degree of active suppleness, impulsion, and lightness of the forehand by self-carriage.

At first sight it would seem that a good novice horse would perform a Second Level test without difficulty, but although the individual movements are easy enough for a well-schooled novice, it is the linking of the movements, and the extra lightness required in the forehand, which will catch out the newcomer to Second Level. To perform a *good* Second Level test, the horse has got to be near, or up to, Third Level in training.

To assist in maintaining the extra collection, Third and Fourth Level tests may be ridden in either a snaffle or a double bridle, whereas lower levels are always ridden in a snaffle.

To sum up, schooling up to First Level consists of the following:

1. Relaxation
2. Correct gait and rhythm
3. Free forward movement
4. Straightness
5. Suppleness — correct bends
6. Correct attitude, including head-carriage and willing acceptance of the bit
7. Improvement of the basic paces to "working" trot and canter

Second and Third Levels, or their equivalent, Intermediate and Open Levels in Combined Training, will require:

8. Further improvement of the paces, to include collected and medium trot and canter
9. Further suppling of the horse, to enable smaller curves and circles to be ridden at all paces (including counter-canter), and to start on lateral work
10. Increased lightening of the forehand, by engagement of the hindquarters, and progressively raising the head and neck

These last three items will form the subject of the next chapters.

Chapter 2

Improving the Basic Paces

THE PACES now universally employed in dressage can be defined as follows:

The basic paces are walk, trot, and canter. The horse, either alone or without interference by his rider, may be said to produce a "natural" pace. As has been said, the natural paces of a horse moving free will be at first considerably hampered by the introduction of the rider's weight to his back. The first step after relaxing the horse must be to restore the freedom of the natural paces. This must be done by increasing the drive from the hindquarters without hampering the horse with the reins. Any attempt to flex the neck at too early a stage would result in shortening and paralyzing the paces.

Fig. 1
Horse moving free,
showing natural trot

Fig. 2
*Natural paces hindered
by weight of rider*

Fig. 3
*Natural paces restored,
light contact of reins,
no attempt to flex the poll*

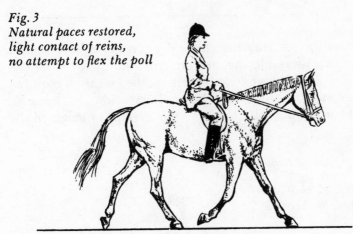

Once the natural pace is restored, the rider can begin to establish the "working trot" — defined by F.E.I. as a pace

between the collected and the medium trot, in which a horse, not yet trained and ready for collected movements, shows himself properly balanced and, remaining "on the bit," goes forward with even elastic steps and good hock action. The expression "good hock action" does not mean that collection is a required quality of working trot. It only underlines the importance of an impulsion originated from the activity of the hindquarters.

Fig. 4
Working trot — poll slightly
flexed, hocks well engaged,
no shortening of natural stride,
the steps active, elastic, lively

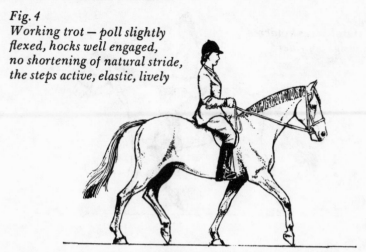

From the working trot, the rider can move both toward more extension into the medium trot and toward more collection. The two are complementary; the extension required in the medium trot cannot be produced without the energy stored up in the collected trot. To attempt to lengthen the

Fig. 5
Horse on the forehand
and "running," hocks out
behind. Flexion of
the poll has been lost

stride merely by giving the horse the reins and increasing the pace will result in throwing the horse on to the forehand and producing the fault known as "running."

Schooling at this stage will include a great deal of change of pace, "fore-and-aft," in straight lines, the horse being constantly asked to lengthen the stride and then to "come back" to the rider for a few paces in slight collection, lengthen again, and so on. Instant response to the aid to go forward is essential. The rider must be careful to watch whether the horse is becoming tired, and not to ask too much. Any tendency to irregularity or loss of rhythm will be a clear indication that the rider is making too great demands on the horse. Other signs of trouble are the horse forging* or going "wide behind."

This type of work is better done in the open country rather than in an enclosed space, where the horse may appear to become bored by constantly going round and round. However, I am not convinced that the concept of "boredom" is correct when applied to horses; I believe that often when a rider says, "My horse is getting bored," it is the *rider* who is getting bored, while the horse is merely getting *tired*. The horse is a creature of habit, and once he can be persuaded to accept a situation, repetition does not affect him in the same way as it does a human being. We must be careful of the dangers of anthropomorphism — that is, the attribution of human sentiments and characteristics to animals.

The rider must not expect dramatic or rapid improvements in the paces. Sudden changes may sometimes come with the removal of a mental block in the horse's brain, but the fact is that improvement of the paces will largely be a matter of better *muscular* development — and muscles can only be built up slowly. However, the removal of mental obstacles can be helped by capitalizing on any of the instincts of the horse which may work in the rider's favor. For example,

* Clicking the front shoe with the hind.

most horses will go more freely when working toward home, or toward other horses, or in company; it is therefore sensible to use this factor to help the horse toward greater effort, if that is what is required. We all know the feeling when a sluggish horse suddenly "perks up" and gets "on his toes" when he sees another horse approaching, and wish we could find the key to producing at will the same effect in the dressage arena, where many horses seem to go "dead" under the rider, whose nerves are probably inducing a similar rigidity in the horse!

Work in the open, particularly up and down hill, will greatly assist the horse in this adjustment of fore-and-aft balance expressed in the rounding of the back; the rider must work consistently, always asking a little more than the horse is inclined to give, retaking and collecting the energy, and, above all, persuading the horse to adopt an exact rhythm and tempo as a matter of habit. It means that there will never be a dull moment during the ride, however uninteresting the scenery, since the rider's mind should be continually concentrated on every step that the horse takes — which will be either right or wrong. The rider's balance must be delicately maintained, since the slightest false move will result in unbalancing the horse and the magic will be lost. Work periods should be interspersed with rest and relaxation on a long rein.

The medium paces at trot and canter require a clearly visible degree of extension.

The F.E.I. definition gives medium trot as

> between the working and the extended trot, but more "round" than the latter. The horse goes forward with free and moderately extended steps and an obvious impulsion from the hindquarters. The rider allows the horse, remaining "on the bit," to carry his head a little more in front of the vertical than at the collected and the working trot, and allows him at the same time to lower his head and neck slightly. The steps should be as even as possible, and the whole movement balanced and unconstrained.

It is worth noting that in the "directive ideas" (i.e., what the judge is to look for) on the judging sheet, the medium trot has the direction "the extension and balance."

The accompanying pictures will help to show the difference between working, medium, and extended trot.

Fig. 6
Working trot

Fig. 7
Medium trot, the neck perhaps a little too high

Fig. 8
Extended trot

Fig. 9
Collected canter

Fig. 10
Working canter

Fig. 11
Medium canter

Fig. 12
Extended canter

In the medium canter there must be a lengthening of the stride without hurrying. The F.E.I. definition includes exactly the same wording as in the definition of medium trot — moderately extended strides, the neck a little longer and lower, the face more in front of the vertical.

In the extended paces — not at first required — the horse

covers as much ground as possible. Maintaining the same rhythm, he lengthens his strides to the utmost, without losing any of his calmness and lightness, as a result of great impulsion from the hindquarters.

The important point in changing pace from working to collected or medium is that the rhythm and tempo (i.e., the rate of the footfalls) must not vary — there should be no hurrying into extension, nor should there be any loss of tempo when collecting the horse.

A word now about the outline — that is, the attitude of the horse as seen from the side — in particular the attitude of the head and neck.

The horse in his natural paces under the rider will normally carry his head without flexion at the poll, with the face angled at about 45° to the vertical. With increasing collection the angle of the face will be gradually reduced until at extreme collection (i.e., in piaffe or passage) it will be very nearly vertical. At the same time the neck will be progressively raised.

Fig. 13
Head-carriage at
working trot

Fig. 14
Head-carriage at collected trot

Fig. 15
Head-carriage at passage

Some faults of head-carriage are illustrated below:

Fig. 16
Face a little too vertical
(at working trot),
a slight fault but a
very common one

Fig. 17
Overbent — a bad fault,
hard to cure

Fig. 18
Above the bit — unschooled
horse

Fig. 19
Neck too short and high,
back hollow, and horse
behind the bit

The head must be steady throughout — there must be no movement, no snatching at the bit or shaking of the head; the mouth should remain closed, and the tongue invisible. Particular care must be taken that the horse does not throw up his head during transitions, and that in downward transitions he does not lean on the rider's hand and throw his weight on the forehand. The judge will be even more critical of these details at Second Level than in lower grades, where minor faults of head-carriage may be treated lightly. But when collection is being demanded, there must be no signs of resistance.

At First and Second Levels the rider has only to show one degree of pace — the working walk, trot, or canter — but at Third Level the rider will be required to show "collected," "medium," and "extended" paces. The difference between these must be clearly shown, not only in comparison with each other, but also in isolation. That is to say, if a horse has a poor medium trot, the rider may attempt to make it look better by shortening the collected paces. The judge must look at each pace in isolation and say to himself, "If I were looking at this pace without having seen anything else, would I know what it is meant to be?"

The point is that the paces must be recognizable to the

judge — and if the judge is in doubt, then the pace may well be less than satisfactory. This is the first main difference that the rider must face at this standard: the clear demonstration of the paces when collected, working, medium, or extended.

Remember that the paces will form the foundation of the judge's marks throughout the test. If the horse has poor paces he will get only poor marks, even if the circle, or whatever else is required, is accurately performed.

This should explain why the marks of 9 and 10 are so rare; unless the paces are correspondingly good, the whole movement cannot be considered as "very good" or "excellent."

Finally, it must be realized that the establishment of correct "working" paces is the foundation of all further training. Those who have watched that great trainer of show-jumpers, Bertalan de Nemethy, will have been struck by his insistence on a well-balanced working trot as an essential requirement before the horse is asked to jump. So often, riders ask young horses to jump before they have reached the necessary standard on the flat. Those who have the patience to wait until the horse is accepting the bit, with a rounded back and hocks well engaged, will find that jumping training is far easier, and in the end will be much quicker.

As already mentioned, at Second and Third Levels it is not only the paces themselves that must be improved, but also the transitions between them. These must be performed with much less progression than at First Level — that is, the horse is expected to halt from the trot, to trot directly from the halt, to canter from the walk, to walk from the canter, and to come from medium or even extended trot to collected trot. Each test will contain nearly as many transitions as there are movements, so that there will be plenty of opportunity to lose marks if the transitions are not good. The horse that is "onward bound" — leaning on the rider's hand, and not carrying himself with a light forehand — will soon be in trouble, especially in the canter movements.

The task of establishing a balanced canter will be of the utmost importance; the work (already mentioned earlier in this chapter) at change of pace will apply equally to the canter. In the next chapter the valuable exercises in leg-yielding will assist the canter strike-off, and in lightening the forehand generally.

Although the rein-back is not included in tests at this stage, it will be required at Third Level, and is most valuable in exercises to lighten the forehand. The rider who finds difficulty in making the transition from canter to walk will find that the sequence canter — trot — walk — halt — rein-back — walk — canter, ridden on the circle, with the halt performed at the same spot each time (on crossing the center line or at the end of the school) will be of great help. The horse soon comes to prepare himself for the halt, engaging the hindquarters in readiness for the downward transitions. The rider can avoid undue anticipation by varying the canter lead, changing on to a circle on the opposite rein, and by sometimes halting without rein-back.

The use of the counter-canter (discussed in Chapter 4) will help not only to supple and straighten the horse, but also to indicate progress in the balance of the canter. The rider at Second Level must feel completely in control at the canter, able to slow down at will without losing impulsion, with the consequent danger of falling back into the trot. Only when this standard of control is reached can the rider hope to get the horse to settle lightly in the downward transitions — and until this stage is reached there is no hope of reaching marks of even "sufficient" value.

Chapter 3

Toward Collection

IN WORKING TOWARD COLLECTION, the rider must remember that all authorities agree that collection imposes a great strain upon the horse; the work must be done slowly and gradually in order to allow the hindquarters and hind legs to become accustomed to the extra load. The rider must think in terms of years rather than months — after perhaps a year's work to reach fair First Level standard, one would expect a further year or more to get the horse into Second Level, another year before reaching Third Level, and at least a fourth or fifth year for Advanced.

The F.E.I. defines the collected trot thus:

> The horse, remaining "on the bit," moves forward with his neck raised and arched. The hocks, being well engaged, maintain an energetic impulsion, thus enabling the shoulders to move with greater ease in any direction. The horse's steps are shorter than in the other trots, but he is lighter and more mobile.

The back is rounded, the joints of the hind legs are flexed to a greater extent, and the paces gain in "cadence" or springiness.

The judge will look at the hind legs to see that the energy is maintained. The result of shortening the stride without loss of energy should be that the feet are raised more from the ground, while bringing the hocks under the body will lighten the forehand.

The collected trot is always performed sitting. In the collected walk, and collected canter, the rules apply — a shortening of the stride, without loss of energy from behind; a slight raising of the neck to lighten the forehand, and to give "increased mobility," the steps being energetic and slightly higher. The horse should give the impression of contained energy, not just of being held in a particular shape.

To bring the horse into collection, the rider must take positive action. Merely to tighten the reins to pull the head in would have the effect of slowing down the horse and shortening the stride, with loss of energy, while the horse would be most likely to resist by leaning on to the bit. Collection is obtained by riding the horse into the bit from behind. The action by the rider is called the "half-halt," defined as an

> almost simultaneous, coordinated action of the seat, the legs, and the hand of the rider, with the object of increasing the attention and balance of the horse before the execution of several movements or transitions to lesser and higher paces. In shifting slightly more weight on to the horse's quarters, the engagement of the hind legs and the balance on the haunches are facilitated . . .

This is perhaps a somewhat clumsy description of the movement — in which legs and seat drive the hocks farther under the horse's body, while the hands, softly restraining the forehand and preventing increase of speed, cause the horse to raise the neck and lighten the forehand. The horse is thus ridden into the bit, rather than pulled back by the reins. The term "half-halt" is regarded with some suspicion in British dressage circles. Continental judges and instructors often say that we do not make enough use of the half-halt. The British sometimes criticize the German school for their half-halts, as being too obvious and exaggerated; one has heard the phrase "the Pull-and-Push School"! Certainly if a half-halt is too visible it is inelegant and may interrupt the free forward movement of the horse. The accent in British dressage has for a long time been on ease and grace of movement, invisible aids, absolute insistence on regularity and evenness at all paces, and an absence of apparent effort. Continental judges often seem to our eyes to tolerate unevenness and irregularity, created in the rider's effort to produce a greater degree of collection, whereas to Continental eyes our horses often lack sufficient collection.*

It is a question of finding a balance and, in competition, of knowing one's judge. Some judges will prefer more collection than others, and their remarks on the test sheet will indicate their feelings to the competitor — who will take more or less notice of what is said!

The pendulum of taste will always swing slowly from side to side. Twenty-five years ago, British dressage was in a state of confusion. Even at Pony Club standard, riders were being required to show extended trot, and, in general, all the early tests were far too difficult. Under the guidance of Colonel and Mrs. V. D. S. Williams, order was restored, and a sensible and logical series of tests was devised, with the emphasis on gradual progression in training, never overtaxing the horse, and introducing fresh movements into tests at the appropriate stages. In America a similar task was performed by the A.H.S.A. Dressage Committee.

At the same time a serious misunderstanding clouded the development of British dressage: only three degrees of pace were used over here — "collected," "ordinary," and "extended." The Continental subdivision into four — "collected," "working," "medium," and "extended" — was not adopted; and to make matters worse, the Continental "medium" trot and canter was translated into English as "ordinary" trot and canter. In tests, therefore, at levels demanding medium trot with some degree of extension, only "ordinary" trot was asked in Britain, while the *same phrase*, "ordinary trot," was used in easier tests in which the Continental riders were showing "working trot." This misapprehension, which continued for nearly twenty years until finally corrected in 1974, has undoubtedly helped to hold back the development of dressage in Great Britain, and must be partly responsible for criticisms such as that of a well-known foreign trainer,

* Unfortunately borne out by British placings in the 1976 Olympics!

who once said, "British riders always look as if they were sitting up there afraid something was going to happen!" Another said, "The trouble with the British 'ordinary trot' was that it was *too* ordinary." I understand that a similar situation existed in the United States.

It is to be hoped that, once the requirements of working and medium paces are thoroughly known to riders and judges, British dressage will improve at an even faster rate than it has up to date. All tests have been rewritten and the old categories of "ordinary" trot and canter have been abolished — broadly speaking, being replaced by "working" trot and canter in Preliminary and Novice tests, by "working" or "medium" pace in Elementary tests, and by "medium" pace in all higher tests.*

Riders must, however, realize that there is no fixed standard of "working" pace — the standard required in Elementary tests would naturally be higher than in Preliminary or Novice tests. The pace depends upon the *work* required of the horse at that stage, more elasticity, energy, and cadence being required as the horse progresses in ability.

Another very important factor in the work on the paces, especially collection, must be both the conformation and the temperament of the particular horse. It is easy enough to generalize about these matters, but the rider is riding one horse, with his own ability and character. There is no doubt that the English Thoroughbred, beautiful mover as he can be, does not accept domination by the rider in the same way as the specially bred Swedish and German horses, and often seems to find collection more difficult.

Every horse and every rider will find obstacles and problems inherent in the physique and temperament of animal

---

* British standards and the U.S. equivalents are as follows:

Preliminary	= Training Level
Novice	= First Level
Elementary	= Second and Third Levels, or Combined Training Intermediate
Medium	= Third Level
Advanced	= Fourth Level

and man, and of both in combination. Perfect results in practice may turn to ashes in the tension of public performance. There is no horse, however, which cannot be improved by correct training and, while one cannot "make a silk purse out of a sow's ear," even quite common horses with limited natural paces may, if trained on sound lines, and improved to the limit of their capability, acquit themselves well against more aristocratic animals.

Chapter 4

Improving Suppleness

SECOND AND THIRD LEVEL TESTS demand greatly increased suppleness in the horse, 8 and 10 meter circles at the trot and the canter, counter-canter loops, and shoulder-in.

The movements of the tests are put together in such a way that a rider who cannot make full use of the arena, going as deeply as possible into the corners at all paces, will be short of time and space in which to prepare the horse from one movement to the next.

The extra lateral suppleness required will form an important part of the horse's schooling, and will bring a dividend, in that improved lateral suppleness will also help the horse to achieve the "vertical" suppleness, obtained by rounding the back, needed for collection.

The groundwork for lateral suppleness will have been laid in the early stages of training, but it is very unwise to embark too soon upon lateral movements requiring collection, since, once the horse learns to move sideways away from the leg, it may well use its extra sinuosity as an evasion from straightness. The rider must therefore be sure that the horse is really going straight at all paces, with free forward movement, with sensitive response to the aids to go forward, before embarking on lateral work.

According to the F.E.I.:

1. The aim of the lateral movements is
    a. To improve the obedience of the horse to the . . . aids . . .
    b. To supple all parts of the horse . . . increasing the freedom of his shoulders and the suppleness of his quarters, as well as the

elasticity of the bond connecting the mouth, the poll, the neck, the back and the haunches;

c. To improve the cadence and bring the balance and pace into harmony;

d. To develop and increase the engagement of the quarters and thereby also the collection.

2. At all lateral movements — with the exception of leg-yielding, in which the horse is bent only at the poll — the horse is bent uniformly from the poll to the tail and moves with the forehand and the quarters on two different tracks.

3. . . . the bend or flexion must never be exaggerated so that it impairs the balance and fluency of the movement . . .

4. . . . the pace should remain free and regular . . . impulsion is often lost, because of the rider's preoccupation mainly in bending the horse and pushing him sideways.

5. Lateral movements should be . . . interrupted by some energetic movement straight forward . . . to maintain or increase the impulsion.

6. . . . the side to which the horse should be bent is (called) the inside. The opposite side is the outside.

7. The lateral movements comprise:

Leg-yielding	Travers (head to the wall)
Shoulder-in	Renvers (tail to the wall)
Half-pass	

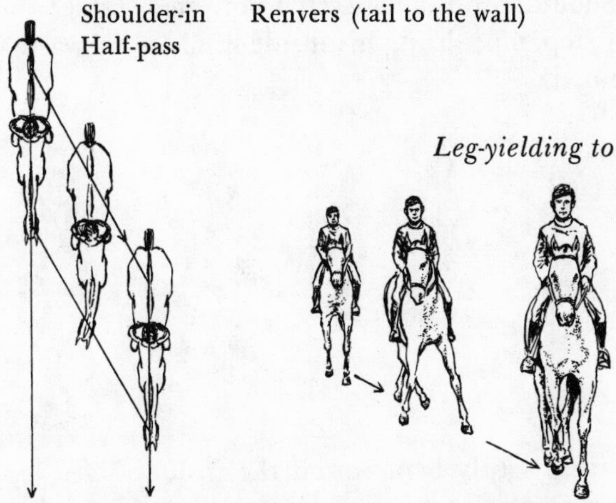

Fig. 20
Leg-yielding to the left

The horse is quite straight except for a slight bend at the poll, so the rider is just able to see the eyebrow and nostril on the inside. The horse looks very slightly away from the direction of movement.

Fig. 21
Left shoulder-in

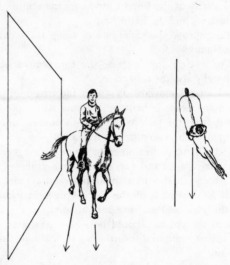

The horse is slightly bent round the inside (left) leg of the rider. Shoulder-in is a collecting movement, since the horse, at every step, must bring his inside hind leg forward and under the body.

Fig. 22
Half-pass left

The horse, slightly bent round the inside (left) leg of the rider, is moving forward and sideways away from the outside leg. The horse is almost parallel to the original direction of movement, though the forehand is always slightly in advance of the hindquarters.

Fig. 23
Controlling the quarters in half-pass

a. *Correct*
b. *Quarters leading — a bad fault*
c. *Quarters trailing — horse hardly on two tracks at all*

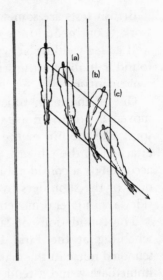

Fig. 24. Travers

Fig. 25. Renvers

Travers and renvers are not required till Third Level; they require more bend and collection than the other lateral movements. It is sometimes hard to remember which is which! Try the following mnemonic: *T*ravers = *T*ail-in; *R*envers = *R*ear on line.

British tests are somewhat cautious in introducing lateral work. Continental tests include lateral work at the walk, as well as leg-yielding at walk and working trot; both will be found valuable in the schooling of the horse for the lateral movements proper.

One of the main functions of lateral work is to free the movement of the horse's shoulders. The shoulder is not a joint like the hip or the elbow, since the shoulder blade is attached to the rib cage only by a pad of muscle. There is accordingly a considerable possibility of improving the freedom of the shoulders by the stretching action forward and sideways in lateral movements.

The foundations of lateral work will have been laid in schooling at the First Level stage. When riding an un-schooled horse in the manège, or closed school, the rider will immediately find a tendency to "fall in" at the corners, the horse dropping inward with the inside shoulder, and looking outward at the same time.

Fig. 26
Horse "falling in"
in the corner

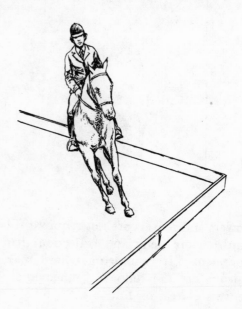

This is the natural tendency for the horse, but it cannot be allowed in dressage, since it is impossible to place the horse accurately in corners or circles. The horse falls out of balance, and would be unable to describe any circle of less than about 20 meters in diameter. The horse must remain upright and be bent to fit the curve on which he is traveling.

The first action the rider must take is to make the horse responsive to the rider's inside leg, so as to prevent the horse from cutting the corner and taking the wrong bend.

Fig. 27
Well-ridden corner

A valuable exercise will be "enlarging the circle," in which the rider making a circle of about 10 meters diameter (at the walk, at first) applies the inside leg in order to send the horse outward into a spiral, until the circle is 20 meters in diameter. Extra work should be done on the horse's stiff side.

The turn on the forehand will assist in teaching the horse to move away from the rider's leg (drawn slightly back) and to cross the hind legs one over the other while turning. A full turn should not be attempted at first, but when the horse crosses his hind legs, he should be at once sent forward.

Fig. 28
Enlarging the circle

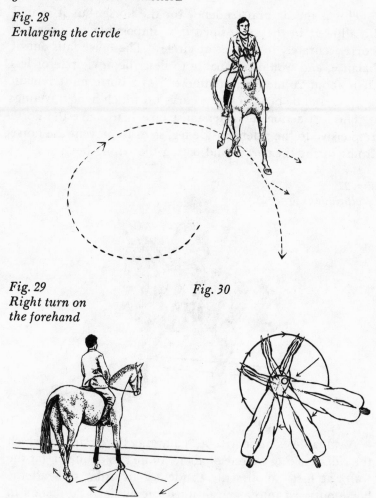

Fig. 29
Right turn on
the forehand

Fig. 30

The rider is applying the right leg, the horse moves his hindquarters away, crossing the off-hind over in front of the near-hind, and turning on the off-foreleg, which remains exactly on the same spot. The horse is slightly bent to the right. The left rein prevents the horse from stepping away with the forelegs. The off-fore (the "pivot" leg) should not remain still but should "mark time" on the spot, maintaining the sequence of the walk.

The rider can also practice putting the horse into "position right or left," by asking the horse to take a slight bend to right or left in the neck and poll while the rider's inside leg prevents the horse from falling inward, and the outside leg sustains the forward impetus; the horse goes straight on.

Fig. 31
Position right and left

Once the horse is responding to these three exercises, riding in the corners ceases to be a problem. Approaching the corner, the rider puts the horse into the appropriate position right or left, keeping the horse straight in the track with the inside leg. The horse will then go round the corner on his own, the strength of the rider's inside leg determining the depth into the corner that the horse will go.

The F.E.I. gives as a guide at collected paces (i.e., including canter) :

> the horse should describe one quarter of a circle of approximately 6 meters diameter at collected and working paces, and at medium and extended paces one quarter of a circle of approximately 10 meters diameter.

This is the counsel of perfection, for the advanced horse. The rider at all standards must put the horse deep enough in the corners only to get round without loss of balance or rhythm. It is a bad mistake to try to corner too sharply; not quite as bad as cutting the corners with the wrong bend, but one which will lose marks nevertheless.

Even at Training Level, the horse should *never* be wrongly bent — there can be no excuse for this fault; at Second and Third Levels, the horse should be able to go really deep into corners at collected and working paces; but at medium trot and canter, rather more space must be permitted.

When the horse is accepting a bend readily to right and left, without coming "off the bit," and when he is responding to the rider's leg by moving the quarters away from the drawn-back leg, then he is ready to make a start on leg-yielding, provided, as said before, that he is moving freely forward.

Riders often find difficulty in coordinating the hand and leg aids for the lateral movements, especially if the movements are first attempted in the constriction of the arena. I believe that the best place to start on lateral movements is in a quiet lane (well away from traffic). The road stretching away in front imparts a natural tendency to the horse to go forward — vital to lateral work, since the forward impetus must *never* be lost, and the horse must never be felt to be going more sideways than forward. If a suitable road is not available, then try working alongside a straight hedge in a field.

The work may be started at the walk, since most riders find it hard at first to apply the aids and stay "with the horse" at the sitting trot. It will also be much easier for the horse, which will be more relaxed at the walk. Stiffness and tension are fatal for lateral work.

The rider, taking advantage of the horse's natural tendency to return to the track or the side of the road, rides parallel, a meter or two out; then, keeping the horse straight, applies the inside leg (in this case, the right) and moves the horse back to the track "on two tracks."

The distance is gradually increased and, when the horse is

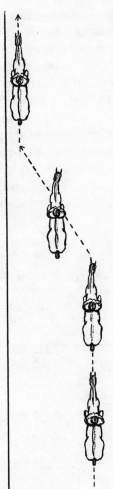

Fig. 32
Lateral work — first steps
in leg-yielding

responding to the aid on either rein, the rider may try moving from the track inward and then back again.

Note that the bend, away from the direction of movement, is minimal — only just enough to show the rider the eyebrow on that side.

When the horse is moving freely away from the leg at the walk, without resistance or tilting of the head, the rider may attempt the same movements at the trot (sitting). The horse will probably find the movement more difficult, and will at first tend to stiffen and to lose impulsion. The rider must be patient and ask for only a very little at a time; two steps of relaxed submission are better than yards of resistance.

The directional guidance of the road will help the rider to keep the horse pointing in the right direction, and will help the horse to keep going forward. Needless to say, the exercise must be performed only well away from any risk of traffic!

Some useful exercises using leg-yielding in the school are shown below:

Fig. 33. Leg-yielding exercises in the school

   (a) *Half-circle and return to the track*
   (b) *Half-circle and leg-yielding to opposite track*
   (c) *Zigzag*

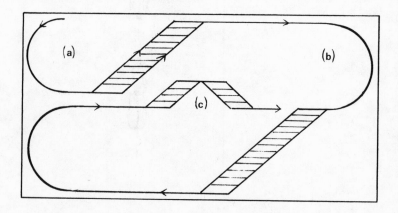

Remember that the bend in leg-yielding is minimal. A slight lateral bend at the poll is enough; there must be no tendency for the neck to be pulled round to either side.

Fig. 34
Leg-yielding as an exercise for the canter strike-off. At E turn
right at trot — a few strides leg-yielding to the right — canter left

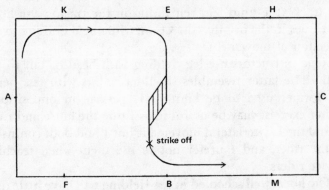

This is a valuable exercise to assist the canter strike-off, loosening the left side of the horse, before striking off with near-fore leading.

From leg-yielding it is a short step to shoulder-in, the only lateral movement required at Second Level.

The difference between the two movements, which seem superficially alike, is as follows:

In leg-yielding there is no collection, the horse is practically straight and moves away from the rider's inside leg on two tracks: The bend is minimal, only a small lateral flexion at the poll being required.

In shoulder-in the horse is more collected, and slightly bent throughout his length. The most important factor is the way in which the inside hind leg is brought forward under the body — a movement which greatly aids collection and the engagement of the hindquarters. If the horse is straightened and released from shoulder-in, he will at once produce a longer stride — an exercise which will aid the rider in working for extension.

In the early stages of lateral work, riders often find difficulty in keeping the horse pointing in the right direction. Personally, I prefer that in leg-yielding the horse is kept straight and parallel to the original direction of movement — i.e., parallel to the sides of the school or manège, whereas in shoulder-in the forehand of the horse is brought in off the track (the hind legs remaining in the track); the horse continues in the original direction, while held oblique to the direction of movement.

Some instructors use leg-yielding with head or tail to the wall. The latter resembles shoulder-in but with less bend; the former used to be known as "passage in opposition." Either exercise may be useful in assisting the horse and rider to find the key to lateral movement but I find both confusing to the rider, and I prefer not to use them when teaching novice riders.

The horse well schooled in leg-yielding will have little difficulty in performing the shoulder-in and, later, the half-pass.

Opinions vary as to the amount of angle required in shoulder-in. The F.E.I. recommends that the foreleg, seen from the front, is aligned with the opposite hind leg, as shown below.

Fig. 35
Left shoulder-in with sufficient angle.
The horse has hardly enough bend

This is often referred to as the horse moving "on three tracks," to my mind a tiresome and misleading phrase. If the angle is increased too far, I have heard it referred to as "four tracks" — an even worse misnomer!

Fig. 36
Left shoulder-in, angle much larger,
horse with too much left bend: the bend
is mainly in the neck, and the outside
(off) shoulder is falling out

If the angle is increased too much, the movement becomes labored, and the forward impetus will be lost. The F.E.I. suggests about 30° as an ideal angle.

The most important point is that the horse must move freely and without strain, maintaining the length of stride, with the inside leg thrusting firmly forward under the body. At an angle less than "three tracks," the hind leg will probably not cross over and the hindquarters will be moving straight forward, while the neck is bent inward — a movement of little value, in which the hindquarters are doing nothing.

The rider should not attempt an angle greater than can be ridden with ease and fluency. If too small an angle is shown, however, the judge may have difficulty in deciding whether the horse is really performing the movement.

In the school, the shoulder-in is usually performed on the long side, or on the center line, when the *hind* legs must re-

main in the track. The shoulder-in is often used in conjunc-
tion with circles — the rider going into a circle or volte (6
meter circle) — directly from the shoulder-in.

Fig. 37. School exercises for shoulder-in

    (a) *Shoulder-in and 10 meter circle*
    (b) *Shoulder-in on short side and through corner, followed by*
          extension
    (c) *Shoulder-in on center line and 8 meter circle, continue*
          straight on at shoulder-in, hind legs remaining in the track

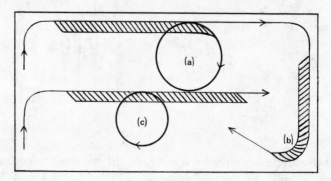

The rider should bear in mind that the pirouettes, which
are performed at walk, canter, or piaffer, are also lateral
movements. The walk pirouette is, in fact, developed from
a half-pass in a very small circle, with the horse bent in the
direction of the turn. The horse schooled in lateral work
will have no difficulty with this movement.*

Fig. 38
Quarter-pirouette at the walk

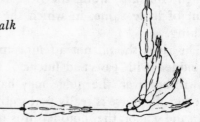

* The turn on the haunches is similar to the walk pirouette, but is not,
like the latter, performed out of a collected gait. It is not used in Britain.

Once started on lateral work, the rider will find school work much more interesting, since there is an opportunity for greater variety of figures and movements. Performing lateral movements correctly will give the rider the feeling of great control of the horse — especially by the rider's ability to "place" the horse exactly while on the move, to correct errors in circles and serpentines, and by the power to increase the drive from the hindquarters. Above all, the increase in lateral suppleness will produce a more tractable, better balanced, and maneuverable horse.

The effect of lateral work, especially leg-yielding, in overcoming resistance, in softening and suppling the horse, can be quite remarkable; riders in this country would do well to study its use. While leg-yielding is at present not in favor with the establishment, its inclusion in the new F.E.I. rules must surely indicate more emphasis in the future.

Another valuable suppling exercise is the counter-canter. In this movement, the horse, cantering in a circle to the right, is deliberately kept by the rider on the left canter-lead; i.e., with the near-fore leading. The rider uses the aid for the canter left (right leg back) to keep the horse on the left lead.

The F.E.I. definition states:

> This counter-canter is a suppling movement. The horse maintains his natural flexion at the poll to the outside of the circle, in other words is bent to the side of the leading leg. His conformation does not permit his spine to be bent to the line of the circle. The rider, avoiding any contortion causing contraction and disorder, should especially endeavour to limit the deviation of the quarters to the outside of the circle, and restrict his demands according to the degree of suppleness of the horse.

The novice horse should be worked in the open, when first attempting the counter-canter, since there is not enough room in the average school or small arena. As the horse gains in suppleness and in balance, the radius of the curve can be decreased, until the Second Level horse can canter round the

Fig. 39
Counter-canter — circle to the
right — slight left bend maintained over
the leading leg (near-fore), which is just
coming forward

end of the small arena on the outside lead; that is, a half-circle of 20 meters diameter. The Third Level horse should be capable of a three-loop serpentine, the full width of the large arena, without change of leg at the canter.

A good counter-canter should be hardly perceptible; the horse should flow on smoothly and without effort. Any signs of laboring or of hurrying indicate stiffness and resistance, and will be penalized in competition.

Chapter 5

Extensions

IN LATER TESTS we shall find the extended walk, the extended trot, and the extended canter. Certain features are common to all three paces:

— the horse must remain straight and balanced
— the paces must remain regular
— there should be no apparent change of rhythm or tempo
— the horse's neck is allowed to become longer
— the face will be slightly in front of the vertical
— the strides will become longer, the horse covering more ground
— the extension must come from the power of the hindquarters

Common faults are:

— the horse, overtaxed, loses balance and rhythm, rolls from side to side, or takes uneven steps, or goes wide behind
— the extension is produced by artificially throwing out the toe on the front legs, without a corresponding activity and length of stride with the hind legs

The most difficult of the three to judge is the extended walk. In F.E.I. rules there is no "working walk" — only collected, medium, extended, and free walk. Up to Second Level tests, the "free walk on a long rein" is required, in which the horse must be allowed to stretch the head and neck, out and down, relaxing in a "pace of rest" (as defined by F.E.I.).

In the extended walk, however, the rider allows some lengthening of the neck, but must retain contact with the reins. The neck goes out, but not far down; the horse must be seen to walk with more energy and to "cover as much ground as possible." If the extended walk takes place on the arena's diagonal, it can be very difficult for the judges in front or behind the horse to detect much difference in the stride.

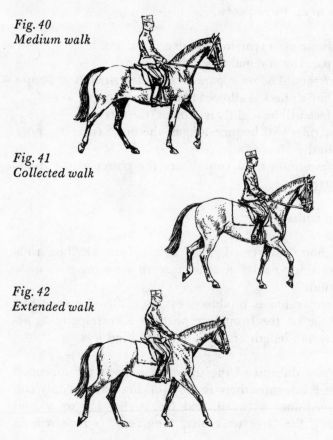

Fig. 40
Medium walk

Fig. 41
Collected walk

Fig. 42
Extended walk

Fig. 43
Free walk on a long rein —
contact by the weight
of the rein only

In the extended trot, the spectator (and the judge) may be misled by an exaggerated action of the forelegs, not matched by a corresponding driving action of the hind legs. Seen from the side, the front and hind legs in each diagonal should appear to remain parallel.

Fig. 44
Correct extended trot

Should the hind leg not be producing the drive, the front leg will be extended in the air, and will then come slightly backward in its return to the ground. This is false, and is a bad fault — but is not always easy to detect.

However spectacular the extension, if it is gained at the expense of regularity it is faulty and will be penalized. It is

Fig. 45
Faulty extended trot —
hind leg movement does
not match the front legs

better to produce less length of stride, keeping the impulsion of the hindquarters in proportion to the general forward movement, smoothly and without hurrying, than to push the horse too far and out of balance. Extension is always followed by a transition downward to collected or working paces, and the horse must be in perfect balance if this transition is to be achieved smoothly.

Similarly, in the extended canter, the horse must be seen to be "giving everything" without undue haste, and yet again must be in balance for the downward transition at the end of the movement.

Schooling for extensions can never be hurried; to achieve them requires the development of the right muscles and the right balance. I was once approached by an M.F.H. who said, "I don't want to learn dressage, but can you teach me to do the extended trot?" He evidently thought that there was some secret aid, which, if applied to his heavyweight (and not very well-bred) hunter, would cause it to burst out into a spectacular progress around the show ring! Extensions can come only from the release of muscular energy stored up in collection, combined with the horse's earnest desire to go forward at the signal of the rider's aids.

Chapter 6

Judging at Second Level

As MENTIONED BEFORE, the degree of strictness for the judge will increase as standards get higher, but the judge must avoid becoming increasingly carping and difficult to please. Faults may be easier to find, but praise and encouragement must not be driven out. However, faults due to wrong schooling — crookedness, stiffness, irregularity, pulling, opening the mouth, and so on — must be punished severely, whereas slight lapses in head-carriage, loss of balance, or momentary loss of impulsion may still be regarded as less serious at this stage.

All judges have slightly different approaches to their problem. My own method is to try to establish a level of marking for each pace, according to the quality of that pace, and then to superimpose on that level the marks for movements and transitions at that pace. Thus, if I consider that the horse has quite a good working trot, I shall start with the figure of 7 in mind — and add or deduct marks according to how the movements at the trot are performed. In the case of faults, the amount taken off will depend on the seriousness of the faults that occur. One must be prepared for a pace to improve or deteriorate as the test goes on, and not necessarily to remain at a fixed standard.

A commentary on Second Level Test No. 2, following the judge's train of thought, may be helpful in illuminating the working of one judge's mind! The horse we will consider will be a three-quarter-bred Event horse, competently ridden by a rider with quite good position and influence. Right and left refer to the rider's right and left, not the judge's view. The small diagrams show the track that the rider should take. In this test the large arena is being used, though the test could be ridden in the small arena.

Fig. 46. Movements 1 and 2

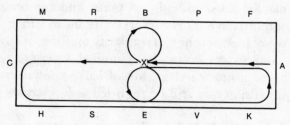

Test	Directive Ideas

(1)

A Enter, working trot (sitting)	Entry (straightness)
X Halt, salute	Halt (immobility)
Proceed working trot (sitting)	Transition from halt

The entry is straight, but coming into the halt the horse tilts his head to the right and resists. The halt is straight, but the hind legs are not square; the horse is still during the halt. Moving off, the horse comes off the center line for the first three strides.

The trot seems rhythmic, but not particularly lively or elastic.

Judge's thoughts — Working trot seems quite nice — not much chance to see it yet; say, a basic 5 or 6. Some resistance into halt, move-off crooked, halt straight but not square, immobility good: 4 would be too hard perhaps.

Judge's comment — *Resisting into halt, off-line moving off: 5*

(2)

C Track to the left	Correctness and regularity of the circles
A Down center line	
X Circle left, 10m diameter followed immediately by circle right 10m diameter	The bearing and flexion of the horse

Plenty of time to assess the trot while the horse goes down the long side. Tracking to the left, the horse is well bent in the first corner; the trot improves as the rider overcomes the nervousness at the first entry. Basically worth 7. Now for the two circles: the first circle is quite good but the rider makes the mistake of crossing the center line at a slight angle instead of facing absolutely straight to C at the change of rein. As a result the second circle is not quite round.

Judge's thoughts — Two main things to mark here: the basic pace, which is worth 7, and the circles. The error in the latter means a loss of one mark at least.

Judge's comment — *Change of rein at X not straight; second circle not round: 6*

Fig. 47. Movements 3, 4, and 5

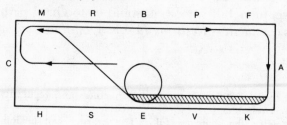

(3)

C Track to the right
M-F Lengthen stride in trot (rising)
F Working trot (sitting)

The lengthening of stride
Maintenance of rhythm
Balance and transitions

The aim will be to lengthen the stride without hurrying or changing the tempo. In this case the rider does not get much response and the lengthening of the stride is hardly visible.

Judge's thoughts — Well, I can't say I saw much lengthening there. Not very easy to see, with the horse going away from me, but I can't say it was "sufficient."

Judge's comment — *Lengthening hardly recognizable: 4*

(4)

K-E Shoulder-in

E Circle right 10m diameter

Balance and flexion in the shoulder-in
The bearing of the horse

The rider comes through the corner A nicely, and the horse starts the shoulder-in well, but nearing E stiffens and throws up his head. The rider is slightly distracted and rides the circle 1 meter too large.

Judge's thoughts — Some resistance there and the circle too big. Two faults, neither very serious. The shoulder-in started well, but was not sustained.

Judge's comment — *Resisting, then circle too large: 5*

(5)

E-M Change rein across half arena
Lengthen stride in trot (sitting)
M Working trot (sitting)

The lengthening of stride
Maintenance of rhythm
Balance and transitions

The shoulder-in and circle should prepare the horse well for the lengthened strides, because of the engagement of the inner hind leg in the shoulder-in and the balancing of the horse needed for the 10 meter circle. In this case, all goes well, and the horse shows a good lengthening of stride. The return to normal working trot at M is achieved with a smooth half-halt, followed by a well-ridden corner.

Judge's comment — *Nil: 8*

Fig. 48. Movements 6, 7, and 8

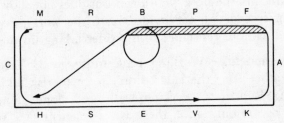

Movements 6, 7, and 8 repeat movements 3, 4, and 5 on the other rein. The horse is now going more freely, and lengthens stride better (7), but in the shoulder-in the rider fails to keep the angle constant ("varying angle": 4), loses impulsion in the circle (4), and then lengthening stride across the arena asks too much and the horse becomes uneven (4).

Judge's thoughts — A typical example at this level of what happens when one movement goes wrong, immediately influencing what follows. However, the rider has now got the walk movements in which to regain composure after that fluster.

Fig. 49. Movement 9

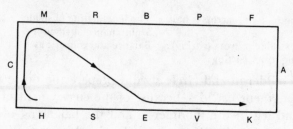

(9)

C Working walk	The regularity of the walk
M-E Change rein across half arena	The lengthening of stride and
Free walk on long rein	frame of the horse
E Working walk	

The working walk is well on the bit. In free walk the horse stretches the neck well down but does not show much swing or freedom in the stride. At E the working walk is regained without resistance to the rider taking up the reins.

Judge's thoughts — Working walk quite good. Free walk was rather lazy; the rider didn't seem to risk asking for much. Return to working walk well done. Since the walk occurs only once, there is a coefficient of 2 on this movement.

Judge's comment — *Free walk rather lazy but transitions good:* $7 \times 2 = 14$

Fig. 50. Movements 10, 11, and 12

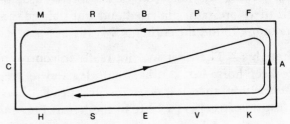

(10)

K Working trot (sitting)	The canter depart
A Working canter left lead	The lengthening of stride
F-M Lengthen the stride in the canter	Maintenance of rhythm
M Working canter	Balance and transitions

In the strike-off the horse throws up his head and cuts the corner after A, with the result that he is not straight on the long side during the lengthened strides till after passing B.

Judge's thoughts — A bad strike-off, and then crooked — at this level almost "fairly bad" — but the rider corrected well, the return to working pace at M was not too bad, and the lengthening of the stride was clearly shown. The working canter itself is perhaps a little hurried and on the forehand; basically worth 5 or 6.

Judge's comment — *Head up striking off, then quarters in: 4*

(11)

H-X-F Change rein, at X change of lead through the trot	The balance
	The transitions

At this standard not too many strides of trot should be necessary — say, not more than four. I prefer the rider to show the same number of strides before and after X; in any case the transition must be smooth, straight, soft, and forward all the time.

The horse falls into trot two strides before the rider is

ready, thus putting the horse on to his forehand, and the strike-off is therefore rather flurried and unbalanced, resulting in a scramble round the corner at F.

Judge's thoughts — The rider was not really in control then, failed to keep horse between hand and leg and to prepare for the transition, then lost direction and headed into the corner instead of keeping a little to the left of F to ensure a smooth corner. All resulting from the canter not being quite in balance.

Judge's comment — *Fell into trot early, transition on forehand: 4*

(12)

K-H Lengthen stride in the can-   The lengthening of stride
ter

A repeat of the lengthened strides, successfully carried out for 7. The rider has the canter more under control.

Fig. 51. Movements 13 and 14

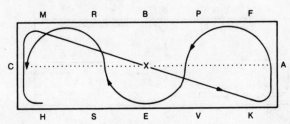

(13)

M-X-K Change rein, at X change   The balance
    of lead through the trot   The transitions

Repeat of the change of lead through the trot. Much better this time: 7.

(14)

A-C Serpentine in three loops   The regularity and shape of the
    width of arena   loops
Change of lead through the trot,   The bearing and flexion
    each time crossing the center   The transitions
    line

In the large arena the loops are 20 meter half-circles, thus allowing plenty of space and making the loops easy to measure. A movement demanding balance and control, and real obedience to the aids.

In this case, after the first transition the horse strikes off wrong, but the rider senses it at the first stride and corrects immediately; the second change goes well with only two strides of trot.

Judge's thoughts — Had all gone well I should have given it 8, but the wrong strike-off must be penalized at least 2 marks. I did admire the calm and quick reaction by the rider.

Judge's comment — *Wrong strike-off well corrected: 6*

Fig. 52. Movements 15 and 16

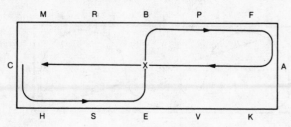

(15)

C Working trot (sitting)	The regularity of the working trot
E Turn left	
X Halt (6 seconds)	The transitions
Proceed working trot (sitting)	The halt (immobility)
B Track to the right	

Both turns at E and B are well executed. In the halt the horse is straight and still, but the hind legs are not square — one leg is left behind.

Judge's thoughts — Horse not quite ridden into the halt again, so the hind leg is out behind.

Judge's comment — *Halt straight but not square: 7*

(16)

A Down center line	The straightness
G Halt, salute	The halt (immobility)
Leave arena free walk on a loose rein	The relaxation in the free walk

This time the horse comes squarely into the halt with all four legs: 8.

Collective marks and comments

Gaits (freedom and regularity)	6 × 2 = 12 Paces rhythmical, but rather limited at present
Impulsion (desire to move forward, elasticity of the steps, relaxation of the back)	5 × 2 = 10 Lacks elasticity and spring, canter rather stiff and on forehand at times.
Submission (attention and confidence; harmony and lightness and ease of movements; acceptance of the bit)	7 × 2 = 14 Obedient and calm, profile well maintained, head steady.
Position, seat of the rider, correct use of the aids	6 × 2 = 12 Rider sits well but did not always prepare horse in time for next movement, and did not always keep horse between hand and leg.

In 16 movements the horse scored 100, giving an average of 5.8.

The collective marks (without coefficient) average 6, so the judge is really saying the horse and rider are basically better than the test marks show — a very common state of affairs at this level, where the extra difficulty of the test will provoke mistakes.

The judge was perhaps in a kind mood, and seemed to be looking for the good points rather than dropping heavily onto the mistakes, no bad thing. In a championship, one could expect to be more critical of detail than in a local club competition, where standards between horses may be more variable. But we should remember that it is not doing competitors a good turn to give them better marks than they deserve. The truth, however unpalatable, is what we should seek, but it should be sweetened with encouragement and helpful remarks. Also, nothing annoys competitors more than a row of bad marks without comments to explain them, as they feel they are working in the dark. Competitors tend to rate judges very much by the sense and helpfulness of their comments, rather than by the marks they give!

The judge at any standard may well be called upon to pronounce upon a world-famous rider who comes in and puts up an indifferent performance, not only on a young horse, but even sometimes on a well-known winner. This situation frequently arises when one judges Combined Training, either at Horse Trials or in classes of dressage with jumping. It is important not to be overawed, to have the courage of one's convictions, and not to feel, because one is watching a rider or a horse that has a great reputation, that either is necessarily putting up a good performance!

Personally, I find that once the horse is in the arena, I am totally oblivious of the rider on top. Whether it is one of my own family, an important person, or an Olympic medalist makes no difference, since my whole attention is concentrated upon the horse and what I am going to say about it, with the result that at the end of the test I find I have sometimes failed to give nearly enough thought to "the position and seat of the rider, and correct application of the aids." To quote General Viebig, a famous German judge and trainer, "A good judge has to view the performance as a whole."

It is often difficult to award the marks to the rider. For instance, if the rider sits well but the horse goes badly, the judge can hardly award very good marks to the rider. Sometimes a well-known rider may produce results well below standard, on seeing which the judge may feel diffident about criticizing someone whose standard of riding is far above the judge's own ability.

Probably the best way of judging the rider is to look for faults of riding which are causing faults in the horse. The most common are: unsteady seat and hands, stiffness in the hands and arms, wrong placing in the saddle, rider leaning forward, reins too long, rider's leg wrongly placed in applying the aids, rider using hands rather than legs to control the horse, and so on. If such obvious faults are visible, then the judge should comment on them. Very often a parent or trainer comes to the judge afterward and says, "I was delighted with your remarks about my competitor — I have been telling her the same thing for weeks, but she won't take any notice." While it is not the judge's duty to give riding lessons, yet attention drawn to a visible fault, combined with constructive suggestions, will do much to soften the disappointment of poor marks, and may help the rider to improve before the next appearance in the arena.

If no faults in riding are visible, but the horse is going badly, it may well be that the results would be even worse under a less skillful rider, but while rewarding tact and skill, the judge's verdict must not contain too much guesswork. Conversely, when a horse goes well under an inelegant rider, the judge must consider whether it is going well because of, or in spite of, the rider! I well remember presenting my son's rather difficult Event horse in a Novice test with Mrs. V. D. S. Williams as judge. The horse went badly, getting a string of 4s — while I got 6 for my riding. I worked on the horse all the summer while my son was away at Sandhurst, and rode before Brenda Williams again some months later. The horse got 6s all through the test, but I got 4 for my riding!

Chapter 7

From Second to Third Level

ALL AUTHORITIES agree that the step from Second to Third Level — or, in Britain, from Elementary to Medium — represents a much larger advance in the demands made on the horse than the differences between any of the lower levels.

The main difference at Third Level is in the basic paces. Working trot and canter are eliminated, and the collected trot and canter become the foundation paces of the test, with the competitor required to show two degrees of extension, medium and fully extended paces, at both trot and canter. In walk, collected, medium, and extended paces are all required.

The purpose, as defined on the back of the test sheets, is "to determine that the horse has acquired an increased amount of suppleness, impulsion, and balance, so as to be light in hand and without resistance, enabling the rider to collect and extend its gaits."

Suppleness is further defined in the A.H.S.A. rules as:

the physical ability of the horse to *shift the point of equilibrium smoothly forward and back as well as laterally* without stiffness or resistance. Suppleness is manifested by the horse's fluid response to the rider's restraining and positioning aids of the rein and to the driving aids of leg and seat. Suppleness is best judged in transitions.*

The other additional movements required at Third Level are all directed toward the goal of improving suppleness, both vertical and lateral; i.e., smaller circles and voltes, work

* A.H.S.A. *Supplement to Rules on Dressage and Combined Training,* amended to 1975, p. 38, author's italics.

on two tracks in all three forms (half-pass, travers, and renvers), counter-canter, rein-back, and transitions from walk to canter, canter to walk, thus introducing the simple change of leg through walk.

Comparison of these requirements with Fourth and the F.E.I. Levels will at once show that although there are more movements to be added to the horse's repertoire — i.e., flying changes, canter half-pass, and pirouettes at Fourth Level, and piaffer and passage at the international level — yet the basic standard for the horse at Third Level is not very different from that of the advanced horse.

A glance at the contents of Third Level Test No. 1 without detail will tell us what we have to face:

Movement No.

1	— Entry, collected trot, salute, and move off
2, 4	— Medium trot across diagonal
3 ⎫ 5 ⎭	— Shoulder-in, 8m circle, shoulder-in as a continuous movement, repeated on both reins
6	— Extended trot (sitting) across diagonal
7	— Halt, rein-back, medium walk
8	— Extended walk across diagonal
9, 10	— Half-turns on haunches at medium walk, canter from walk
11	— Medium canter on long side
12, 13 ⎫ 16, 17 ⎭	— 10m canter circle, simple change of leg on to counter-lead, 20m circle in counter-canter (on both reins)
14	— Medium canter on long side
15 ⎫ 18 ⎭	— Extended canter on long side
19	— Extended trot (sitting) across diagonal
20	— Collected trot with halt on center line at L
21	— Halt at G, salute and exit

Examination of the layout of the test will show that the medium trot is all in straight lines; the lateral work comes early in the test and provides the only movement of any technical difficulty. Both medium and extended paces are demanded for the full length of the large arena. These long sustained extensions are very different from the few "lengthened strides" required at lower levels; therefore our horse must be going freely enough, and with sufficient impulsion to sustain these paces *on his own* without needing a lot of drive from the rider.

There are over thirty transitions in this test (counting simple changes and halts as two); therefore if the horse is not supple enough to perform these smoothly, softly, and straight, there are going to be plenty of opportunities to lose marks!

It is axiomatic that a horse at Third Level is straight at all times, stands square and still in the halts, and since the basic trot and canter work is at collected paces, the horse must go really deep into the corners. Any faults in this respect should provoke severe treatment from the judge. It is far away from the stage when horse and rider can come into the arena and scratch around just following the track of the movements; the rider has got to show the paces clearly defined for what they are — collected, medium, extended; the horse must be straight as a ramrod on straight lines, and show supple bends in the curves. The head must be still, the mouth closed, the angle of the face always in front of the vertical, but the poll must be flexed so that the forward impulsion from the hindquarters can be softly absorbed and contained in the rider's hand, through the mouth and the reins.

At this level, unsteadiness of the head, snatching at the bit, dropping behind the bit, holding back above the bit, or over-

Fig. 53. Shoulder-in followed by circle

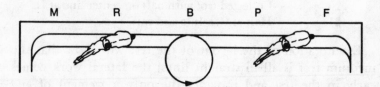

bending should be punished even more severely by the judge
than at lower levels.

It may be interesting to look at the series of movements at
3 and 5, where the rider has to show shoulder-in followed by
an 8 meter circle, continuing in shoulder-in.

This is, in fact, a classic training exercise for suppling the
horse and engaging the hindquarters. When the horse is being taught the shoulder-in, at the first sign of resistance he
should be sent forward into a circle (larger than 8 meters)
and brought back to the track. In this movement, the 8
meter circle is more difficult than the shoulder-in, and the
judge will be looking for any signs of loss of rhythm or impulsion, the roundness of the circle, and the horse remaining
steadily on the bit.

The other difficult moment in this test is at movements 12
and 16, when the horse, after a 10 meter circle at collected
canter, is required, on returning to the track, to perform a
simple change on to the counter-lead; i.e., with the outside
foreleg leading.

Fig. 54. Change to counter-lead

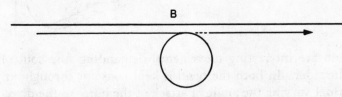

This is a good test of obedience since the horse's natural
inclination is to strike off with the inside foreleg in the
school. The rider will be wise to practice this strike-off on
the counter-lead frequently, and in different places around
the arena. It is not easy to remain perfectly straight during
this simple change.

The 20 meter counter-canter circle which follows at the
end of the arena should present no difficulty to the Third

Level horse — indeed, I would expect a good novice horse to be able to perform it without effort, although it is not required in tests at that level.

The lateral work in Third Level Test No. 2 is also interesting — on the long side shoulder-in, 8 meter circle followed by haunches-in (travers) ; the rider then turns down the center by a half-circle of 10 meters and performs a half-pass back to the track.

Fig. 55. Circle followed by haunches-in

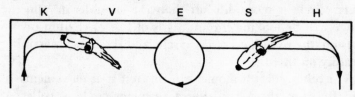

Fig. 56. Half-circle followed by half-pass

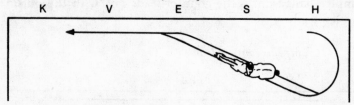

Both are interesting movements, demanding fine control by the rider. In both the bend is kept constant throughout, the rider varying the angle of attack of the horse to the direction of movement. The lateral movement has to be sustained for a very long time, so lightness and full impulsion are essential.

Opinions among judges vary as to the amount of bend required in the two-track movements, where the bend is *toward* the direction of movement — i.e., half-pass, travers (haunches-in) , and renvers (haunches-out) .

In the half-pass the bend must be definitely shown and maintained throughout the movement. Loss of bend is a very bad fault. If not enough bend is shown, the movement merely approaches leg-yielding. The more advanced the horse, the more collection and bend can be shown.

If the half-pass is performed as the horse comes toward the judge, nearing the side of the arena, the bend becomes more difficult to see, and the judge may think the rider is losing it. Therefore my advice to riders is to make sure that the bend is clearly visible to the judge — too much is better than too little!

Both the travers and renvers require more bend and collection than the half-pass.

The F.E.I. rules give diagrams of correct and incorrect positions of each of the lateral movements, leg-yielding, shoulder-in, travers, renvers, and half-pass. These are well worth studying, since they give good guidance as to the amount of angle and bend for each movement. They are shown below and on the following page.

Fig. 57
Leg-yielding on the diagonal

Fig. 58
Leg-yielding along the wall

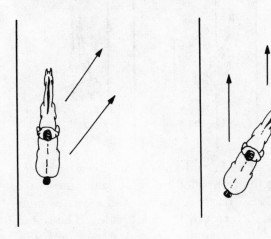

Fig. 59
Shoulder-in correct

Fig. 60
Shoulder-in incorrect

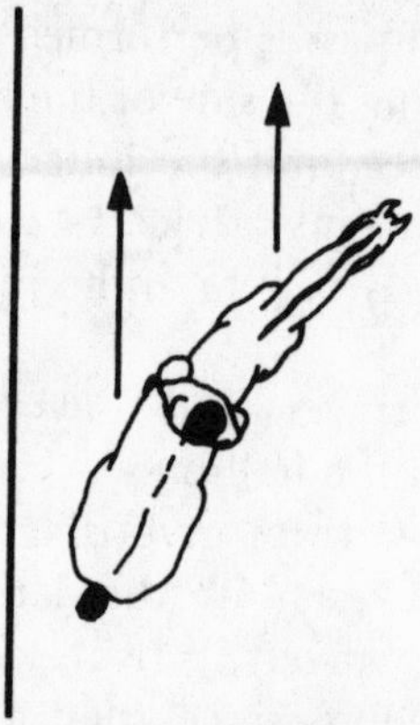

Fig. 61
Travers correct

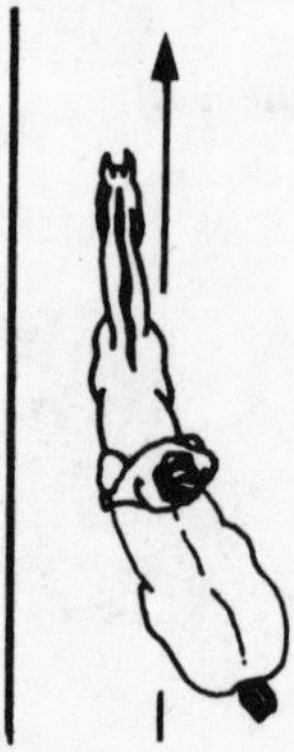

Fig. 62
Travers incorrect

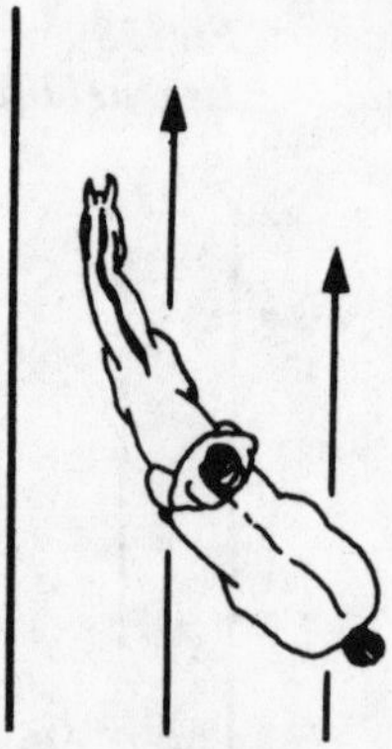

Fig. 63
Renvers correct

Note that in shoulder-in and travers the horse is placed only so as to bring the front foot on to the same line as the opposite hind foot, i.e., "on three tracks," and a greater angle is definitely cited as incorrect by the F.E.I. rules. The rest of Third Level Test No. 2 contains no greater technical difficulties; there is a four-loop serpentine in collected canter, full width of the arena, with a simple change of leg at X, creating the equivalent of 15 meter counter-canter circles. The simple change must be made through walk, and will be from one counter-canter loop on to another, a good test of obedience to the aids.

Fig. 64. Four-loop serpentine

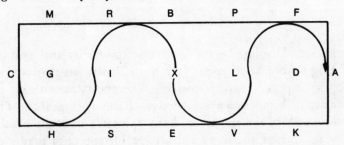

The rein-back, which will be found in all tests from this level upward, will undoubtedly have been introduced in schooling before now, since it will have been impossible to obtain the lightness of forehand, lowering of the quarters, and engagement of the hocks without its use. The rein-back, correctly performed, with a rounded back and flexed poll, is a valuable suppling exercise; but should the horse resist by raising the head above the bit and hollowing the back, the reverse will be true, and the rein-back will be damaging to flexibility.

There is an illustration of the rein-back at Fig. 67 in the Appendix.

Work at this level should give intense pleasure to the rider; the sense of unity with the horse, the horse's ready response to the aids to move forward, sideways, or backward, the lightness and softness of the mouth, the springy comfort of the paces, should, when all is going well, make the rider feel privileged to receive such willing cooperation as a reward for the previous years of work.

Chapter 8

On Watching Dressage

DRESSAGE "displays" — such as those given by the Spanish Riding School, the Cadre Noir, a quadrille, pas de deux, or solo by experts — give pleasure to the spectator without requiring of him* much knowledge of the finer points. The showmanship, the music, and the spectacle have an instant appeal. Indeed, the more knowledgeable spectator may even be the loser, since he may detect technical faults, not apparent to the less expert, which may spoil his enjoyment.

Watching dressage competition, however, is quite different. The solemn silence, the repetition of the same test by large numbers of competitors, the delay in processing and issuing the scores of as many as five judges, all combine to make the task of the spectator a serious matter. There is something of the atmosphere of the slow unfolding of a cricket match, combined with the "compulsory figure" phase of a skating competition. The spectator finds it hard to become involved. Efforts to assist his participation have not been very successful. Illuminated scoreboards are helpful but can be misleading, since the judge may defer or alter a mark; movements carrying "coefficients," in which the scores are multiplied by 2 or 3 (such as piaffer and passage), will not appear correctly on the board; attempts to produce a meaningful commentary audible to the spectators (but not to the competitors) are subject to technical difficulties — a shortage of acceptable commentators, problems of setting up the apparatus, and

---

* The spectator is referred to as "he" throughout, to avoid the cumbersome "he or she," and not through "male chauvinism."

collecting the necessary extra money to cover the cost and to pay the commentator.

The spectator, therefore, is driven to his own resources if he is to become involved in the competition. He must first ask, "What am I looking for?" and, having gained this knowledge by experience or by study, he must apply it and ask, "What am I looking at?"

In Advanced dressage there are a number of movements which the spectator will never have ridden himself, and in which he will never (unless he is a judge) have received any instruction. Most riders with any pretensions to horsemanship will have progressed as far as shoulder-in, half-pass, walk pirouettes, counter-canter; but there are few who can school for flying changes in three-, two-, or one-time, canter zigzags, canter pirouettes, piaffer, passage. The spectator watching these advanced movements must learn the requirements in order to appreciate how well or badly they are being performed. In addition to learning the requirements, which can be done simply by reading the F.E.I. rules, he will greatly increase his pleasure if he learns something of the methods, and the problems, of producing these advanced movements. If he can watch a rider working under a trainer, he will gain interest and insight, and a degree of sympathy with rider, horse, and judge.

Again, his pleasure will be enhanced if he can sit with a judge or a rider and can exchange comments and discuss (in a discreet manner) the movements of the test. Discretion is emphasized, since often at a competition or at a show one finds some "know-all" sitting in the row behind who provides the unlucky crowd around him with an inaccurate and half-baked account of the proceedings, sometimes peppered with slanderous comments on the riders and judges!

The dedicated spectator may also like to devise his own scoring system. It is possible, with one of the little modern pocket calculators and a knowledge of the test, to mark the movements and add the total, though in advanced tests the movements come at rapid intervals, and there are special marks for transitions, coefficients for extended walk, pirouettes, piaffer, and passage, which would turn the whole exercise into something like a touch-typing lesson. The spectator would do better to sit back, watch the whole test through, and allot a single general impression mark to one place of decimals. Thus if the spectator decides that the first test is in the category of "fairly good," varying toward "good," a mark of, say, 7.7 could be allotted. Subsequent tests receive marks on their merit, but if two tests are very close together, then the spectator must decide which he prefers, and allot one a decimal point above or below the other. An order of merit will gradually be built up, which can be compared not only with the collective result achieved by the judges, but also with the marks of the individual judges, which are generally shown on the scoreboard at dressage competitions.

The spectator must not be surprised at any lack of agreement among the judges. It is not unusual for each judge to produce a different winner, especially in advanced classes, where the judges sit at very different view points — one in the center of the short side of the arena, one near each corner on the short side, and one halfway down each long side. Besides differing view points, differing opinions of the merit of the movements often produce considerable variations in marks; but since judging is a matter of opinion, rather than of fact, such discrepancies are inevitable.

On the Continent, in important competitions a protocol judge is often employed. This official does not mark the competitors, but dictates a running commentary on the test. This protocol is made available to the judges, in case of disagreement. It used to be the practice for judges to compare their marks, and in the event of there being a discrepancy of more than two marks, the scores had to be reconciled. This process greatly slowed up the proceedings, adding minutes to the interval between competitors, and hours to the total time of the class. Partly due to the enormous increase in the number of competitors, this practice has been dropped, though judges often do consult each other from time to time. If there is no discussion, the less experienced judge learns nothing from the others.

To return to the spectator who has kept his own scores and produced his own order of merit, there is no reason why, if he finds some wide difference from the judge in his results, he should not, if he gets the opportunity, approach the judge after the competition and ask why so-and-so was marked in such a way. He will certainly receive a reasoned answer. Judges often spend the whole day at their task, shut up in a car* or tent, and it is rather pleasant to find someone who is interested enough to ask questions at the end of the day. Similarly, the judge should always be available to riders after the competition, if they wish to discuss their test.

To help the spectator, brief descriptions and requirements of most of the usual movements are set down in the Appendix of this book, together with some of the more common faults.

A question often asked by spectators is, "How much does conformation affect the marking of dressage tests?" The key to the answer, in my opinion, lies in the fact that the judge has to work by what is seen. A horse of poor conformation will be likely to show bad basic paces; another animal, hollow-backed by nature, will have difficulty in engaging the hindquarters, and both these horses will lose marks accordingly. The powerful build of the Lippizaner makes piaffer and passage easier than for the narrower Thoroughbred, but the latter will have greater facility in extensions and lateral work. At the lower levels of dressage, the judge will find a great variety of animals, stuffy little ponies, common cobs, Thoroughbred weeds, competing against well-bred and naturally well-balanced animals.

* Cars are preferred in Britain owing to the unreliability of our climate and the prohibitive expense of hiring any form of temporary structure for a large number of arenas.

As was said before, the marking will depend first on an assessment of the basic paces as ridden, and then upon the accuracy, fluency, and smoothness of the movements. The horse which has beautiful natural paces, but is unsteady, resistant, disobedient, and so on, is likely to get fewer marks than the commoner animal, which, though it has limited natural paces, is submissive, supple, and shows impulsion to the best of its ability. Sometimes it is more difficult to assess the dull animal, which does not do anything wrong but plods round the arena without much impulsion or elasticity, yet is calm and obedient. This type may end up higher in the order than the judge really likes merely because it does little that is obviously wrong.

On the whole the marking system works out pretty well; if the wrong one sometimes turns out to have won, there is always another day for the loser. The test is designed to prove the training and muscular development of the horse at that particular moment, as seen by the judge, and has not, as in the show ring, anything to do with the market value or potential ability of the horse in the future.

At more advanced levels, the spectator may find free-style competitions (known in German as *Kür* — the word means "election"). In these the competitor, sometimes after a short set test, enters the arena for a time of, say, five minutes, and must perform certain compulsory movements. The rider may arrange these movements in any order. Other movements at the same standard may be included. One minute before the end the bell is rung, to warn the competitor that time is running out, and the test comes to an end with the final bell. Marks are awarded for the compulsory movements and for the general impression of the program and performance. This competition, if at Advanced standard, is much more interesting to watch than the normal tests.

In a Dressage Derby, eliminating competitions over a period of days are used to select four horses with their riders.

These riders, in turn, ride their own and each other's horses in a set test or free-style, after a preparatory period of two minutes in the saddle. Prizes are awarded both to the winning rider and to the horse with the most marks. Though these competitions are popular with spectators, riders do not like subjecting their horses to this type of test, which can therefore be used on only a very few occasions.

In the dressage phase of Horse Trials and Three-Day Events, the standard of test set depends upon the competition. In Britain, the general standard of dressage shown by Combined Training horses is somewhat lower than that of horses engaged at the same level in dressage only. I am, however, assured that this is not the case in the United States.

To sum up — the casual and uninformed spectator at a dressage competition may find little of interest, except possibly at the higher levels, where the more spectacular movements will catch the eye. To the spectator who is prepared to make the effort to educate himself, any competition from the lower standards upward can be interesting; and if good riders and good horses are competing, the spectacle can be delightful.

Chapter 9

Conclusion

IT IS CERTAINLY NOT asking too much to say that *every* riding horse, whatever its eventual purpose, should be trained up to Second Level. It is not a lot to demand that a horse should be supple enough to canter in a circle of 10 meters on either rein, to be able to make the transitions from one pace to another smoothly, to carry himself with light, elastic paces, and to accept the bit with flexion at the poll. There is no "fancy high-school stuff" demanded here; no trainer of novice show-jumpers or novice eventers, no nagsman of good-quality hunters, not even the trainer of young steeplechasers could cavil at these minimum requirements. The extra impulsion and suppleness demanded at Third Level, combined with the ability to perform single flying changes, should be the aim for good show-jumpers, polo ponies, and Three-Day Eventers. Beyond these standards, the rider penetrates into Advanced Dressage, where the horse is unlikely to be used for anything else, largely owing to the risk involved, rather than any other reason.

Throughout this book there is little mention of the rider — "seat, position, and application of the aids." As I wrote in *Dressage for Beginners*, I do not believe that anyone can learn to ride by reading. One must submit oneself to criticism and instruction in order to acquire and maintain a correct seat; once this has become established, the rider will never lose it, though bad habits may creep in from time to time, and physical deterioration from old age or injury may bring difficulties.

Working in isolation is not good for either horse or rider. The horse that is always worked alone will become silly when introduced to the hurly-burly of a show. Hunting seems to have a calming effect on most horses; but if hunting is not available, membership of a riding club and instruction with a class of riders will be equally valuable.

The question often asked is "What is the point of learning dressage; can't I just ride and enjoy myself?" The answer is "Yes, you can, but don't be surprised if you find problems with your horse which you cannot solve!" A horse which is schooled up to Third Level will be a far more pleasant ride. He will be better balanced, more supple, more active, and better equipped for any other aspect of the horseman's art; and he will probably be a great deal fitter too!

The majority of riders may never achieve this standard themselves, nor may they even have the chance to sit on a horse schooled to this level — let alone own one themselves. But those who succeed will have achieved one of life's great pleasures, and will have acquired a skill in training the horse that will last well into old age.

A Spectator's Guide
to Advanced Movements

IN GENERAL — remember that in all movements, at all times, the following faults will incur penalty:

- crookedness
- incorrect gait — wrong sequence of footfalls
- irregularity
- loss of rhythm
- unlevelness or unsoundness
- horse not accepting the bit steadily — pulling, resisting, tilting the head, throwing the head up, etc.
- loss of balance
- loss of impulsion
- stiffness
- inattention
- disobedience to the aids
- coming off the aids

The paces and transitions

The difference between the paces, collected, medium or extended, must be clearly recognizable. In advanced tests "working" paces are not used.

The transitions between the paces must be smooth, soft, straight, forward, and definite. The first stride of the new pace must be a full one. The horse must maintain his outline, with no movement of the head.

The aids

The rider's aids should be as invisible as possible. Exaggerated movements of the rider's body constitute a fault.

Movements on two tracks

In advanced tests these will consist of shoulder-in, half-pass, travers, and renvers, at the collected trot, or the last three in collected canter. In all but the first of these movements the horse is bent toward the direction of movement.

Half-pass

The main points to watch are:

— the ease and fluency of the movement, the horse always going forward without laboring or stiffening in any way, and the steady acceptance of the bit
— the correct bend of the longitudinal axis, particularly at the poll
— the correct placing of the quarters, not leading or trailing too far
— the maintenance of the movement at a constant angle
— that the movements are performed in the same way on each rein

The half-pass is often used in zigzags or "counter-change of hand." In this movement the distance or the number of steps right and left is usually specified in the test; if it is performed at the canter, each change of hand requires a flying change. The rider is faced with the problem of straightness at this moment, for if the quarters are trailing even slightly during the movement to one side, they may be leading after the change.

Travers

The forehand remains in the track, while the quarters are brought in. Rather more collection and bend is required than in half-pass.

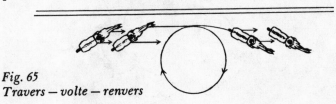

Fig. 65
Travers — volte — renvers

Renvers

The quarters remain in the track, while the forehand is brought in. Again, more collection and bend is required than in half-pass. These two movements are often separated by a volte, or small circle, such as a pirouette.

Pirouette

This movement is a turn on the haunches on the move, without change of rhythm or tempo, loss of activity, or change of sequence of footfalls.

Pirouettes are performed at walk, canter, or occasionally in piaffer. The horse is bent slightly toward the turn.

Ideally, the inside hind leg, which is the point on which the horse turns, should remain on the same spot, but should continue to go up and down in the proper sequence. To remain exactly on one spot is extremely difficult, so it is not wrong for the inside hind leg to move in a very small circle — up to about 2 feet in diameter. Once the circle becomes bigger than this, the competitor is liable to incur penalty, but it is far preferable for the horse to perform the pirouette fluently, but on too large a circle, than to do the movement badly through attempting to turn too sharply.

Fig. 66
Canter pirouette left

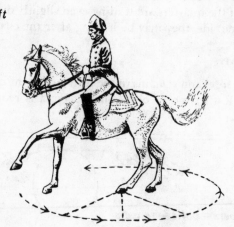

Bad faults are:

— loss of activity of hind legs
— loss of correct footfall
— loss of rhythm
— stepping back
— rearing up
— quarters swinging, resulting in a turn on the center

Fluency and apparent ease of movement are all-important

Rein-back

The horse must be absolutely straight, the steps back must be by diagonals, in two-time* and with full strides. The quarters must be lowered and the head steady, with no resistance. The rider must not be seen to pull on the reins. The number of steps must be exactly as specified; the movement forward again must be a full stride. The horse must not run back out of control. Dragging the feet is also a fault.

Fig. 67
Good rein-back

---

* The new F.E.I. definition says, "The feet are set down almost simultaneously by diagonal pairs."

Changes at the canter

In the simple change of leg the horse is brought directly from canter to walk, takes one or two strides, and then strikes off directly into canter on the other leg.

In the flying change, the horse changes legs in the air, beginning with the hind legs, or the change cannot be completed in one stride. If the change is not achieved in one stride the horse will be said to be "late behind" or "late in front" — both are mistakes, "late behind" being the worse fault.

In tests the number of changes will be specified, and the intervals at which they should take place — e.g., "7 changes of leg every three strides," "15 changes of leg every stride." The competitor will be penalized for any mistakes. For example, in three-time changes the judge counts *one*-two-three, *two*-two-three, *three*-two-three, and so on, while watching for any faults in execution.

These would include:

— crookedness
— swinging the quarters
— unequal length of strides
— faulty footfall
— cramping the paces
— loss of impulsion
— jumping upward

Again, ease of execution is the hallmark of good flying changes, the horse flowing onward with effortless strides, not appearing to interrupt the rhythm, the outline, or the free forward movement in any way.

Voltes

The volte is a very small circle of 6 meters in diameter.

The important points to watch are that the horse is correctly bent, the head is not tilted, that the circle is absolutely round, and that the horse keeps a regular rhythm, with no trace of unevenness. If the volte is slightly too large, it might be considered only a minor fault, provided that the horse shows no signs of stiffness.

Serpentines

These figures are ridden at trot or, more often, in advanced tests, at canter, the number of loops being specified. At the canter, if no changes of leg are demanded, every other loop will be in counter-canter. In the Intermédiare test — just below Grand Prix in difficulty — there is a six-loop serpentine the full width of the arena, with flying changes, arranged to give the first two loops in true canter, the next two in counter-canter, and the last two in true canter.

The judge will watch for the accuracy of the loops, no stiffness in counter-canter, and the correctness of the changes, ridden accurately on crossing the center line.

Passage and Piaffer

The F.E.I. definition of Passage runs as follows:

1. This is a measured, very collected, very elevated and very cadenced trot . . . Each diagonal pair of feet is raised and returned to the ground alternately, with an even rhythm and a prolonged suspension.
2. In principle, the height of the toe of the raised foreleg should be level with the middle of the cannon-bone of the other foreleg. The toe of the raised hind leg should be slightly above the fetlock joint of the other hind leg.
3. The neck should be raised and gracefully arched, with the poll as the highest point and the head close to the perpendicular . . .
4. Irregular steps with the hind legs as well as swinging the forehand or the quarters from one side to the other are serious faults.

The Piaffer is defined as a highly measured, collected, elevated, and cadenced trot on the spot. The horse's back is supple and vibrating. The quarters are slightly lowered, the haunches with active hocks are well engaged, giving great freedom, lightness, and mobility to the shoulders and forehand. Each diagonal pair of feet is raised and returned to the ground alternately, with an even rhythm and a slightly prolonged suspension.

The requirements for the height of the legs are similar to those of the passage, the forelegs coming higher than the hind legs; there should be no swinging of the quarters or forehand, nor crossing of the front legs; the horse must be "animated" by a constant desire to move forward as soon as the aids for the piaffer cease.

Fig. 68
Piaffer — full elevation of legs

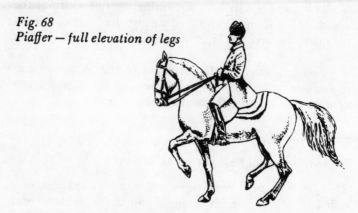

There are only a handful of horses in Britain capable of producing piaffer and passage at all, and few in the world able to achieve, without fault, the maximum heights recommended by the F.E.I. definition.

Fig. 69
Piaffer — moderate elevation

The performance of passage and piaffer varies very considerably with the conformation of the horse. Regularity, ease, and lightness should not be sacrificed in the effort to gain too much height.

Other faults to be noted are:

— loss of rhythm
— unequal height of strides
— moving forward in piaffer, unless specified in the test
— moving backward in piaffer — a very bad fault
— hopping with the hind legs
— double beat with the hind legs

The transitions into and out of passage and piaffer receive special marks in the tests, and the marks for passage and piaffer are often multiplied by two.

Collective marks

In tests of Prix St. Georges' standard and above — i.e., Intermédiare and Grand Prix — the collective marks at the end are doubled in value, and are awarded for the following:

1. Paces — freedom and regularity
2. Impulsion — desire to move forward, elasticity of the steps, suppleness of the back, and engagement of the hindquarters
3. Submission — attention and confidence, harmony, lightness, and ease of the movements; acceptance of the bridle, and lightness of the forehand
4. Rider's position, seat and use of the aids

The judge therefore disposes of 80 marks in the general impression of the test — nearly 20 percent of the total marks.

It is possible that the very high proportion allotted to collective marks at this level is to some extent responsible for the variation in results often shown in judging Advanced classes. If a judge likes the general impression of a horse that has made mistakes in detailed movements, he may nevertheless compensate in the collective marks, and override earlier losses. These differences of opinion between judges in Advanced tests are sometimes puzzling to the spectator; but it should be remembered that there are five judges involved, each with a different view — three at the end of the arena, two at the sides — so that movements such as extended trot or flying changes may look much better from the side than from the head-on view. In international classes judges may come from different countries, with consequent variation of emphasis in the requirements of their national schools. The spectator who has never judged an Advanced class should, however, try to refrain from that worst of evils — uninformed criticism!